THE PORTAGE POETRY SERIES

SERIES TITLES

Dear Lo
Brady Bove

Sadness of the Apex Predator
Dion O'Reilly

Do Not Feed the Animal
Hikari Miya

The Watching Sky
Judy Brackett Crowe

Let It Be Told in a Single Breath
Russell Thorburn

The Blue Divide
Linda Nemec Foster

Lake, River, Mountain
Mark B. Hamilton

Talking Diamonds
Linda Nemec Foster

Poetic People Power
Tara Bracco (ed.)

The Green Vault Heist
David Salner

There is a Corner of Someplace Else
Camden Michael Jones

Everything Waits
Jonathan Graham

We Are Reckless
Christy Prahl

Always a Body
Molly Fuller

Bowed As If Laden With Snow
Megan Wildhood

Silent Letter
Gail Hanlon

New Wilderness
Jenifer DeBellis

Fulgurite
Catherine Kyle

The Body Is Burden and Delight
Sharon White

Bone Country
Linda Nemec Foster

Not Just the Fire
R.B. Simon

Monarch
Heather Bourbeau

The Walk to Cefalù
Lynne Viti

The Found Object Imagines a Life: New and Selected Poems
Mary Catherine Harper

Naming the Ghost
Emily Hockaday

Mourning
Dokubo Melford Goodhead

Messengers of the Gods: New and Selected Poems
Kathryn Gahl

After the 8-Ball
Colleen Alles

Careful Cartography
Devon Bohm

Broken On the Wheel
Barbara Costas-Biggs

Sparks and Disperses
Cathleen Cohen

Holding My Selves Together: New and Selected Poems
Margaret Rozga

Lost and Found Departments
Heather Dubrow

Marginal Notes
Alfonso Brezmes

The Almost-Children
Cassondra Windwalker

Meditations of a Beast
Kristine Ong Muslim

WHERE BABIES COME FROM

"Kind of like Russell Edson, but with more birds and more citrus, and thus with significantly more feathers and significantly less scurvy. Ori Fienberg's debut is gently zany and wonderfully absurd in the best possible ways."

—BRIAN EVENSON
author of *The Glassy, Burning Floor of Hell*

"Paging prose-poem storks: *Where Babies Come From* is proof that a three-parent strategy succeeds, Ori Fienberg's work inventively triangulating Zachary Schomburg, Gabriel García Márquez, and Charles Simic. Stocking his nursery with rusty fogs and psychic ponies—a statue's dust eater making the toy box cut—Fienberg's collection has me reevaluating the outlandish and the heart-toll of wished-for child scenarios, surrealism serving as our oasis 'for ideas that [hover] just out of reach.' The more I read him, the more I want a nation-library underwritten by 'packs of tiny gazelles,' where Ori is laureate."

—JON RICCIO
author of *Agoreography*

WHERE
BABIES
COME
FROM

POEMS

ORI
FIENBERG

CORNERSTONE PRESS
UNIVERSITY OF WISCONSIN-STEVENS POINT

Cornerstone Press, Stevens Point, Wisconsin 54481
Copyright © 2024 Ori Fienberg
Illustrations © 2024 Ainsley Romero
Used by permission of the artist.
www.uwsp.edu/cornerstone

Printed in the United States of America by
Point Print and Design Studio, Stevens Point, Wisconsin

Library of Congress Control Number: 2024942449
ISBN: 978-1-960329-53-0

Cornerstone Press titles are produced in courses and internships offered by the
Department of English at the University of Wisconsin–Stevens Point.

DIRECTOR & PUBLISHER
Dr. Ross K. Tangedal

EXECUTIVE EDITORS
Jeff Snowbarger, Freesia McKee

EDITORIAL DIRECTOR
Ellie Atkinson

SENIOR EDITORS
Brett Hill, Grace Dahl

PRESS STAFF
Carolyn Czerwinski, Allison Lange, Sophie McPherson, Kylie Newton, Natalie
Reiter, Ava Willett

for Emily

ALSO BY ORI FIENBERG:

Interim Assistant Dean of Having a Rich Inner Life
Old Habits, New Markets

POEMS

WHERE
BABIES
COME
FROM

Exhausting Conversation

It begins with the fragrance of silence, a blend of light perspiration and sleep.

The beds shift and bounce, communicating each to each. Sighing with larynx-like springs, messages pass through floors. They were not built for opinions, but they form as naturally as sheets pushed to the bottom of a bed during a warm night. They use us to say the things they cannot say on their own. Sometimes the talking takes all night.

At daybreak they're in exhausted disarray, waiting to have their minds made up again.

Fair Passage

The cave did not lead down into hell. Nor did it ascend into mountains, weaving its way towards hazy angels. Instead, everyone believed it to be a direct passage to a man's heart.

The entrance to the cave was kept open; children often played around the outside and the few who ventured within later described comfortable warmth and a moist rumbling.

Conflating other adages, every evening women would place savory pastries and sweet fruits within; it was unclear whose heart the passage led to, but by morning the food was gone.

Untitled

Everything he touched lost its name. His mother lost hers just as he started his first cry, then the doctor who cut his umbilical cord, his father who held him, and so on.

Dictionaries were no help, so he taught himself to read without words. Each night his dreams were filled with nameless images. When he looked around, he could see something always passing but never returning.

He followed it towards all the places he'd never been, toward names he knew. When he awoke he trailed a glowing orb, looping around with no direction and no end.

Silent Catalog

A woman makes her way through General Fiction starting with A, while a man does the same starting at Z. It takes hours; they must touch the spines of every book, they linger, paying their respects over some, before continuing their journey across names.

Meanwhile, a man dies in the Mysteries section, between E and G. His white-knuckled hands are strangling a paperback book which has done him a terrible wrong. Later, as usual, the night librarian must pry it from his fingers to restock and dust the area so the library can add to its catalog of fingerprints.

They have a book in mind, though they can't remember the author. At last, they meet: their fingers touching the heavily creased spine of the very same book. They smile at each other, but because this is a library, neither speaks.

Gibbous

They followed the trail of crumbs like hungry birds and ate their way across the hall, over mountains of hard-boiled eggs, minced-meat croquettes in tidy pyramids, and steaming rows of pot pies. By the oven the baker labored, back hunched protectively over an enormous tray of moon cookies.

The children are ravenous. They grab greedily at the cookies and eat the dark halves first. They've grown. Their shirts are too short. They yawn loudly. He can read the menu on their pale pot bellies.

At last, they curl up on soft pillows of cheese. As they sleep, the baker seals the children behind a wall of cake. Yet it's always the same; they awaken hungry, and free themselves from their edible prison. The food is gone, so there's nothing to do but smile as they peck out his sweet red heart.

Teething

Following the sound of chewing on the scythe, the farmer found a harvest of granular yellowish porcelain amidst the chafe. She gathered these uncut gems for trade in town.

But teeth had become a common harvest. They found molars at the heart of drupes, eyelets in the place of olive pits, and ears of cuspidic corn. With no single use clear, she traded for a full set, and having heard stories of teeth planted in the ground, plowed, planted, and awaited the rise of legions of warriors.

Instead, a mandibular cliff began to rise. She roped it off, since wherever stands a wall of teeth, it will not be long till someone tries to break them.

Changeling

With a branch cast in silver to use as a key, we steadily circle a whitethorn tree. We circle till we're hungry, then circle till we're tired, till we're irritable, and as the argument begins, we find we've passed over the fairy gate. As it turns out, this is the hard part. We tickle their fancy: we ask for something no one wants: a changeling baby.

To keep up appearances, they demand a tithe in bran muffins and scones. We offer baskets of tiny apples mottled in gold. They demand four winters worth of hot chocolate memories. We ply them with bushels of blueberries and clotted cream, and all the memories of an imperfect apple cider recipe. They tell us the ways that primal beings change, the vital importance of keeping the house clean. But it's a charade: they have so little interest in raising their offspring themselves, that they will only agree if we take twins, and promise not to bring them back.

At home, we review the hastily scrawled instructions: egg allergies, cold hair washes, how as toddlers they grow into different beasts. We gradually soothe disgruntled donkeys to sleep. In darkness, they wake as beavers, gnaw through the spindles, and by morning our hair is in tangles, as our angsty lobsters set about shredding the mattress. Fortunately, they soon begin to strut about, rapidly molting peacock feathers.

Brick Harvest

They are in bloom: pinks and reds, some touched with green fuzz that begs to be rubbed away from weighty fruit. They provide no food or shelter. Their only juice is history.

Rarely do they have the exposure necessary to come into full bloom, and those who covet the properties of aged mortar run off with the finest samples.

Here is another pile: broken pieces masquerading among potatoes, there a storage shed beyond repair. On the horizon, a red sunset walls off the earth from gray rain clouds.

Old Habits

It's a familiar story: a man pushes a boulder up a mountain, when it rolls back down he grudgingly pushes it back up. It's not exciting, but it's steady work, and also the only work available. Eventually, the stone feels like less of a burden, the rough parts smoothed from aeon upon aeon of rolling.

Something rattles from within. It sounds like furniture. It sounds like a chair, a desk, and a bed. Mostly he hears the thump and rustle of books, and within the books he can make out the jingle of fine print, a few bright, sharp notes, like long, thin wind chimes. Something clinks that must be a magnifying glass. He has had plenty of time to be sure; hence, he pushes the boulder carefully, so as not to upset its contents. Eventually, he does the natural thing and burrows into the stone, making himself at home.

Everything is in its place, just the way he heard it. The magnifying glass remains intact, the wood handle smooth, as if from heavy use. He begins reading each book, ready to decipher the fine print. The stone misses its old routine: it continues to roll up and down the mountain, with the man inside.

Winter

Three old men eat oysters in the cemetery. They shuck them from rough and gritty coffins, and then slurp up the delightful corpses.

Something is inside them: misty waves of salt, or sunlight absorbed through dark water. Something is leaving, something necessary, like drops from the ocean, like memories, like tears. Empty oyster shells pile on top of the tombstone of a friend.

Three old men shuffle out of the cemetery together: their smiles are clusters of pearly-white in a sea of gray.

Ride to the Top

There once was a pony. He set up a magic show somewhere in Arizona. There were cards, illusions, levitation, and sometimes even, the pony would read the minds of audience members, sharing their stories with soothing accuracy.

But whenever someone sat down to write about his feats, all they could remember was a rocking sensation, the smell of hay, and the soft creak of wind against wooden walls.

And around this time there was a horse that was making the news, because, you see, she could talk. Someone gave the horse (or perhaps she was a zebra) a tv show, and no one really knows what happened to the pony.

How We Move

The longest game of chess is still underway. It was nearly one hundred years before the first pawn was captured, but lives were shorter then and the players more hasty.

Now it may take a full generation to perform a single move, and so the lineage is passed on with the eldest offspring studying the moves of their ancestors, memorizing the story of each square on the board—a sacred history—before they are given their own unique set and may at last begin to contemplate how petty conflict can change everything.

Some are frozen by the mere possibility and abdicate responsibility to the next generation, while others yearn to make their own singular move to advance family history.

Ancient Wonders

The eyes may be the stained-glass window to the soul, while the lips form a foundation, and a furrowed brow offers something in terms of lift, but the nose is the flying buttress of the face.

It is little wonder that the first Westerners to explore Inuit territories would change the basic architecture of the so-called Eskimo kiss. Somehow the small area of contact when two noses touch and their gentle friction manages to relieve stress on load-bearing lips, pulling them gently up and open.

Gravity and time cause all sorts of havoc, but the tip of the nose is there for us: without its support, the face would collapse, but instead it anchors us in air, slowing our inevitable descent.

The Origins of Masonry

It had been wheat they hoped to grow, to make their bread, but the grain grew into gravel, and then became stones, so they made tidy rows of rock instead. Each spring they planted their seeds and awaited another harvest of rough round fruits.

After a few years the men discovered that they loved the rows. They loved how these simple lines parted different crops, how they marked the beginning of fall, and passing years. Between cracks they added mortar, a mixture of love notes and leftover grain.

Out of this romance, walls were born. These useful children grew up sideways, making their parents proud. Walls have a way of spawning other walls. Soon every family had at least one they tended, reaping safety and separation in nearly equal parts.

Olympic Aspirations

That night, they tore all the metal from the hills. Then they fought. Only when the fogs smelled of rust were they sure they had done their duty. No one had won; it was not that kind of war.

They agreed that the communities along the shore should throw their metal tools of destruction into the lake. Contests celebrated who could throw their spears farthest from the shore. Swords heaved from their tallest ships sliced through the air like leaves angered by fall and then dropped into the water, out of sight.

Fishers woke to find their work completed: schools of fish impaled on currents of spears. Then they dredged the discarded metal from the lake for a new project: the casting of their dreams, one bronze idol at a time.

Night Hungers

He watches from the corners; he watches from the walls. His fingertips are like gentle sandpaper, soft from years of rubbing. His tongue is long and dry, feathery as a new paint brush. All day he smells the museum goers. He can never leave. He is so very hungry.

The different layers of odor wrap around them: that ordinary perfume of the outside, the air disrupted by travel, the dried remains of steam from meals. He knows the way breath smells when words die in the mouth, again and again. This, of course, is another way of measuring time. At night the dust settles. Then the man in the museum comes out. He comes out from the walls. He comes out from the corners. He drifts in from the empty space. He coalesces around a headless statue and eyes the neck.

As he salivates the air becomes dry and still. Then he extends his tongue. He eats the dust off statues and laps lovingly at impressionistic paintings, he tickles tasty tarnish free. All night he feasts so things stay the same. He feasts on newness, but he can never leave.

Ideogram

No keep is complete without a moat, they said, and so they began tracing the outline of their home with a shovel: making it separate, an island of land within a field of land.

The clouds in the distance loom like dark idols: transient monoliths, rumbling with anger or just rain. It is true; you must have the rain, and lots of it to have a proper moat.

But the finishing of a circle goes deeper than water. When it's finished, fear will be conquered through the repetition of a singular letter, a groan, a tone of surprise etched into the ground.

Staying on Track

Like his father, whenever he spoke a new idea, a steam-engine-run train emerged from his mouth. It was possible to spot the idea coming, as his throat would glow and the area around him rumbled slightly. Specialists assured him there was no cause for alarm; it was a mysterious nuisance, but hereditary, and besides, the trains were quite small.

School discussion posed some difficulty as well. Fortunately, it was a well-documented condition, and so accommodation could be made; each room was equipped with a circular track, and he was given extra time to articulate particularly in-depth ideas, which could lead to additional cars, or a tiny, overly-energetic conductor, repeatedly pulling the train's whistle. Some ideas were like that.

It could get overwhelming: all those ideas: all those trains to maintain, or to find bearing down on him in the night. The trains kept irregular schedules, returning the next day, or much larger, years later. His father insisted that one day the trains would take him someplace, though he was vague on the exact details of the location.

Prudence

Everyone walking near the square had a vague feeling, like they'd lost their keys, and they all rifled through their purses and catalogued the contents of their pockets.

Others noted the angel statues were more convincing than usual. Grander wings. They were wreathed in something that couldn't possibly be fire. Some tried to take pictures, but later the pictures came out over-exposed. It was a beautiful day for ideas that hovered just out of reach.

So, they all strode about purposefully, doing very intense window-shopping, but they kept slipping their hands into their pockets, wondering what was missing.

Clockwork Dog

She was attracted by the scent of things turning: the friction of passing and passed time from the clocks we take for granted. She spent hours retrieving discarded bottle caps to bury beneath her favorite windmill.

She was vigilant for the sound of car engines being cranked. Antique weathervanes also piqued her interest, while tornadoes made her apoplectic with happiness: running in joyous revolutions, she'd bark and nip seconds from the most violent edges of time. She slept in city parks and by playgrounds, mesmerized by merry-go-rounds, falling into long dreams where she minded the rotation of planets.

Beneath bleachers she watched arms flip around, waiting for balls to be released. She was hungry for the molecules rubbed off fingertips and the seams of fastballs, but still sated by the perfume of long fly balls.

Where the Bees Are Going

Their yards were full with clover, their gardens with wild flowers. Everyone in the town hummed happily, from sunup to sundown. It was true, what they said about the townspeople: they sang with sweet, strong voices, but when they spoke, they wheezed. It was a slurred and syrupy sound.

One rainy day, everyone in town felt a need to sing. They turned their heads towards the sky, and when they opened their mouths, bees poured forth and became furry, yellow-black, shifting ropes of notes, respected by lightning, rising beyond the clouds. Some townsfolk climbed their ropes, never to be seen again.

The air was thick with pollen when the coroners arrived. They found silent bodies filled not with blood, but with honey. *Ah ha!* said one of the coroners, as though he had just solved an ancient riddle. They sneezed as they cut samples of honeycomb from chests and put them into little jars.

The Death of Typos

The change would probably come gradually: first the homonyms, the misspelled words, and then the dangling modifiers. Finally, the commas slide seamlessly into position.

They are burning erasers in the streets. Grizzled copy editors drink desperately, striving to reach a magical point of intoxication where errors will reappear. Red-pen covered manuscripts of unpublished novels are put into museums.

At last, English teachers will have their reward: they lurk in dark alleyways ready to sell stacks of former students' discarded drafts to fetishistic collectors.

Spare Parts

The store specializes in spare parts for second-hand children. They stock baskets full of hair: long amber locks, springy dark curls, and gossamer blonde waves. Bellows wheezing on a shelf contain the high-pitched utterances of glee: mouth-open shock, unintelligible burbles, and neon colored hiccups following rapid-fire gasps. Our fingers comb bins of button noses, uncork carboys of sibilant cries, and flip through loose-leaf binders on a drafting table as we consider obsessions: from baseball cards to bugs in shoeboxes, or even whether a velvet whiskey bottle pouch for glittering stones would serve a child best.

We have struggled to make a child on our own, in the usual way, so we buy only a paper envelope filled with the dainty sneezes. But once we're home we feel a fresh imperative. We sift through drawers, cabinets, and shelves: surely if a store can sell spare parts, we can make our own child from things we have lying around the house. A small steel mixing bowl for a belly, an old table supplies the legs, miscellaneous cables for arteries, handfuls of rubber bands and twisty ties for ligaments and tendons, and a drawer full of old cellphones to supply its brains. Everything we've saved, all the parts we were sure we'd find a use for some day, we tie, and tape, and yearn together.

Clomping around on wooden legs, her numerous rubber bands twang as she bounds from room to room, exploring her origins: tossing the spare pillow which supplied her downy hair, staring eye-to-eye with a jar of marbles, twisting sinews of pipe cleaners into springs, she's filled with the excitement of being. We're not surprised when she takes a tumble, and we're alerted by a barrage of late 90s ringtones. We soothe her wood-chipped knees with Murphy's oil, and because she may be hungry, we crack two eggs, and place mashed banana and flour in her bowl.

Proper Burial

Each thing we take from the earth requires we bury something of equal value. Dinosaurs buried each other where they fell, feathered and massive. Still later, we bundle whole ships with furs for warmth, and spices to trade beneath the earth. One age buries another, patting dirt upon civilization.

Dogs understand the rules when they bury bones. We bury capsules filled with the fears we hope for most. Sealed coffee cans rattle with the remains of our best morning. In cement-lined pits we bury toxic waste, and then bury our heads in our hands, fingers interlaced, seepage inevitable. But someone always comes eventually to disinter all our ancestors, and more people live now than have ever been buried.

After ages spent polishing handles and blades, the time has come to dig. Start making holes in your yard or park. The beach invites the shovel. Excavate till you find the memory you've buried, transformed by time, pressure, darkness, and ready to be uncovered, cleaned, and tapped for energy.

Facts about Marsupials

When a poem is born it's so small that 40 of them could fit in a tablespoon. It's pink, fur-less, and easy to crush or misplace.

For the first weeks the poet carries them in a tablespoon, day and night, like a continuous egg and spoon race to nowhere in particular. Every now and then, the spoon tips and some tiny poems are lost.

When the time is right, the poet moves the little things to a special pouch, where they stay until they are ready to poke their heads out and consider their own direction.

Making Acquaintance

There was a boy made entirely out of eggshells. He was not nearly as fragile as you'd think. But he was prone to traveling long distances unintentionally.

The shells gradually filled with soil, a little from each spot he came to rest. He developed a warm earthy smell and green hair that he was very proud of.

The more fronds he grew, the less he traveled. Most mornings he sat in the sun and listened to the passing music of pollination.

Limey

She is the daughter of the man who has been stealing limes from the Moon, that inveterate hoarder of lusty, duskened citrus, which it keeps as a proof against scurvy that it fears could strike unexpectedly, causing the Moon to pop from the sky, like an orbiting tooth from the galactic gums.

The limes are hidden beneath the softest silt, and must be approached silently, then coaxed from their sub-zero slumber with phosphorescent entreaties and talk of the sea. Only then can the man pack them into Demerara rum-stained barrels before sliding down the first shoots of dayspring to the ground.

She catalogs and then candies the limes to bet in her monthly poker game with our Sun, which has entered its adolescence and constantly threatens to expand and envelope us all in a maelstrom of fire: but then, what more could a parent wish from its child?

Providence

They were wandering around dressed in human-suits; navy attorney-suits and too-tight hipster-suits. Human skateboards blazed around corners carrying angels in angsty-adolescent-suits.

Every human who approached the square had the vague feeling they'd lost their keys. Most found them quickly. They felt a sense of warmth and elation. But they dismissed it since that's pretty much what anyone feels when they manage to find something after they're sure it has been lost.

A few people really had misplaced their keys, and as they checked their pockets they had the same sense of simultaneous delight and comfort, which was pleasant, but somewhat confusing.

Spring

All the dictionaries have been stolen from the great library. Who could need so many dictionaries?

Researchers wail incessantly because they cannot find the right words and the librarians plug their ears with chewing gum scraped off the bottoms of desks. The scholars are frenzied; ink drips uselessly from their pens. Finally, someone finds a good thesaurus.

Carousal, gaiety, jubilee, revelry, fiesta; merriment, pleasure, bliss, satisfaction: great thoughts can now continue!

Permissible Natures

Just about everyone knows that a goldfish will grow to fill its home, but fewer know that they will die if their hearts mutate too large.

There are no seasons for a goldfish. Their cells are in a continuous state of harvest, but they keep everything they grow for themselves, and so no home can be too large. But we share time as if it were fallen leaves.

Our hearts give and receive over the course of each beat. This is why humans are of relatively stable size.

The Case for Renting

There was a house made of birds. Wood was needed for warmth, and they lacked the funds for brick and mortar, but they had many nets and so each day they hauled in more birds.

It really took considerably fewer birds than they were expecting: birds were very good insulation.

But every now and then the birds would fly off, and when it rained, flapping wings sprayed them. So, they brought out the nets and hauled in more birds until the gaps were filled.

Dream Laureate

For Emily F Maloney

The time has come to wreath a new dream laureate in feathers. A special committee sifts through a mountain of the downy offerings from our nation's foremost dreamers and hopeful amateurs. One of them will help us through this wakeful period, remove the densely packed bags from beneath our eyes, and lead us to a pasture of pillows and possibilities.

I hope, but may not even know if I am chosen. I sent many of the same old dreams as the year before during a last-minute nap, and I did not include a SASE. There are the series of endless flying dreams I had when I was still a child, countered by more recent dreams, where I levitate, just a few inches from the ground, and must balance carefully in the wind before settling several feet away.

But sometimes the old dreams are the best. Like the one where you are typing your essay on the outstretched wings of birds, a murmuration lulled by the patter of keys. Each bird offers us new notes of narrative before taking your pages to the sky. A few feathers drift decisively along unforeseeable currents; one day our child will find this sentence and place it in a drawer for safe keeping.

One More Home Remedy

A gravel pit is filled with many marvels: a perfectly smooth petrified goose egg, or the odd glitter of something semi-precious next to the rusty engine of a split piece of quartz. Gather them in a pouch now, because enough rain and they'll be silt beneath our feet.

We can't resist things that glitter, things that have formed under pressure, small pieces of proof of the way of the world. In this way even the body collects stones.

Try to keep the stones of childhood close. The ones we lose are so much more pleasant than the ones we gain. Jiggle the pouch every now and then to remind your body that you have just enough already. And failing that, always be sure to hydrate adequately.

Strong Man

The heaviest things were easy. He reorganized rivers, he could always keep a secret, and he never cried.

One day he stayed in bed because his sheets were too insubstantial. To rise up, he put tragedy on one shoulder and the sky on the other. With a burnt tree trunk in a notebook made from sheets of drywall he began to collect words.

First, heavy words for light: ethereal, vaporous, and indistinguishable. Later, light words for the heavy: time, love, life, and death.

Spectral Evidence

The students ghost in and out of five-paragraph mausoleums, while their teachers undertake the task of embalming the last remaining argument. They will stay after class, because they are chained to the blackboard, anxiously anticipating the next high tide, another wheeze-filled wave of grading.

Worms writhe spastically through a line of shriveled and fermenting apples perched sloppily on the teacher's desk, which is also where he will sleep at night, naked feet in the breeze, toenails curling, back rigid, arms crossed over his chest.

Meanwhile, he calls up the star pupil, her eyes burning combustible logics into her decomposition notebook. When she reaches the board, she crams her mouth with broken chalk and masticates heartily, expelling white flecks, rather than admit her spectral evidence for the class's judgment.

Sprout

When the results of the X-Ray returned, the boy learned the seeds weren't just in his stomach: thousands floated through his bloodstream, pumped confidently through his heart, cushioned his steps, and, though he earned excellent grades, his brain was mostly seeds.

They had never seen anything like it, but the doctors were unperturbed. We can scoop them out if you like, they said, but it's an elective procedure.

The boy was happy; he drank as much water as he could, wishing for a jungle to play in. Even so, his parents continued to fret, worried birds would sense the prize that lay just beneath the surface of their son.

Midnight of the Caramel Eaters

Long after the muscular pullers of salt water taffy have sunk into their post summer stupor, the mid-autumn moon makes a firm ball in the sky. Its light extrudes softly against cellophane clouds.

It takes all this time for the solstice slurry to be batched, for the fat of the land to mix with clean sweat and certain memories and for the earth to slowly stir. The heat spreads fragrant plumes of mist throughout the sky and then, finally, the air begins to cool and the concupiscent candy, caught at the cusp of the seasons, begins to harden.

The eaters fling handfuls of cubes high above, open their mouths, and begin to chew. Soon tendrils stretch from mouth to mouth; they cannot stop till they are sated, till midnight has passed.

Revolution

One leaf revolted against the rake, and the rest joined in. Piles mobilized, trees shook in sympathy, and bags of clippings spilled into the streets.

Now the leaves are on rampage. The streetlights turn from green to yellow to red, and the armies of autumn are unleashed, scraping the air as they storm down streets, into shops, into restaurants, and into food they refuse to pay for. In parking lots they parachute through open sunroofs, and then there are leaves driving cars down the street, swerving around trees, honking wildly, and colliding with each other. At an intersection a beige car crashes into a maroon car, and then more cars crumple around them, bursting into yellowish orange.

The smell of burning leaves fills the air. Then a strong wind blows and the pile drifts away.

Paleontologists

Beneath their skin most children have dinosaur bones (a very few also have a brain in their behind). Always, the dinosaur in them wants to eat. It stalks about the houses and roars for food.

The inner dinosaur wants to mingle with more of its kind. It gets excited when it goes to museums and sees itself hanging from ceilings.

Very few adults have dinosaur bones beneath their skin (or a brain in their behind). Aging tends to lead toward extinction. Children evolve millions of years at a time, until something happens: an internal ice age, or possibly the meteor of puberty.

Good Grazing

All the young men of the village are put out to pasture. At first this does not please them. They line the fence and bleat for their mothers.

During winter they grow bearded and wooly. As it becomes warmer they butt heads and brawl for days until they realize the pleasures of grazing. On cooler nights they huddle together by a copse of trees. As the first summer storm approaches, they face the wind together. After it has passed, they line up to be shaved.

Fall arrives. One man unlatches the gate and the rest stroll into the village. Then a new herd of young men are led out to the pasture.

A Brief Exploration

Early one evening a man begins an excavation of himself. He sweeps away the cobwebs of recent events, and then lifts the memory chains, till he has access to his inner sanctum.

Then the man wades, waist deep, through chewed, missing caps of a thousand ballpoint pens, up to an ark filled with the sacred relics: fossilized dinosaur bones, vials of honeysuckle nectar; scrabble tiles stacked like gold coins and spilling from burlap sacks. He hears barking from a box of puppies, the first he'd ever seen for sale.

But there's nothing he can bring back, and while he's worshipping in the temple, nothing new can be added. The man replaces the chains, apologizes to the spiders, and leaves, for now.

Mastering an Art

We will have a special award for aging. For rusty faces, bones that grow brittle, and patina covered hands.

Everyone will age as enthusiastically as they can. Some are bound to focus on the amassing of years, but it is not just the most experienced collectors who age best. Also, to be considered is the light unpredictable dust of small things lost, and for the true competitor, the accumulation of some heavier sediment.

The ceremony will be held on a random day every year. It will go on as long as is necessary for everyone to receive their award.

Special Delivery

We go to the delivery room at the hospital and watch the babies through the glass. None of them are our baby: we are just window shopping: at least till we find one we like. We fan out cash on the glass, pointing to the baby we want, but they are not for sale.

After that we continue our usual efforts, heading to the botanic garden, with our nets. We stalk the storks as they return home from all the directions of their deliveries, to a carefully cultivated stand of cypress, where with luscious macro-vertebrates we lure one into our net. Then we secure its wings and put it in the cage with all the other storks: we will interrogate them, feather by feather, beak by beak, till we extract a promise to subvert the supply chain and redirect their precious cargo to our home.

The storks stay silent; their union is too strong. One squawks something about Amazon, so we order a baby online, for next day delivery; twelve hours later, an unmanned drone sails, stork-like through the clouds, and deposits one cloth-swaddled package on our doorstep, C.O.D. Then we apologize to the storks and set them free.

Infrastructure

After years of planning by the foremost poets, only votes in the House and Senate remained; then, at last, they could begin work on the national sonnet. Coney Island and former farmland in NH began preparing bids for verses, while the final couplet would be written on the Mississippi River.

Others protested the sonnet fiercely, insisting that the construction of a sonnet was best left in the hands of private contractors, or at least that each state should construct their own sonnet. Some suggested that the government could never complete the sonnet in a timely fashion, and that after repeatedly extended deadlines, a villanelle was far more likely, or even that the whole project would devolve into rambling blank verse.

Many politicians vowed to block the bill, on the basis that if a multi-year national poem project was begun, at the very least it should be in an American form. A bipartisan coalition against rhymes promised a filibuster; each member taking turns till they recited the entirety of *Leaves of Grass*.

The Sweetness

When humans evolve, in many millions of years, towards flight, the primary adaptations will occur not at the arms, but in the ears. Only the ears are primed by a proper understanding of the vibrations of currents.

Recently scientists discovered the lasting effect that song has on surfaces it makes contact with. Indeed, this change occurs on a quantum level and is cumulative. All sorts of wells contain the nectar of residual sounds.

In Brazil there have been reports of hummingbirds alighting just above a person's shoulder. Those who have experienced it describe a tickle so soothing that it plays along the inner ear like a warm whisper, a living q-tip; the feeling of song.

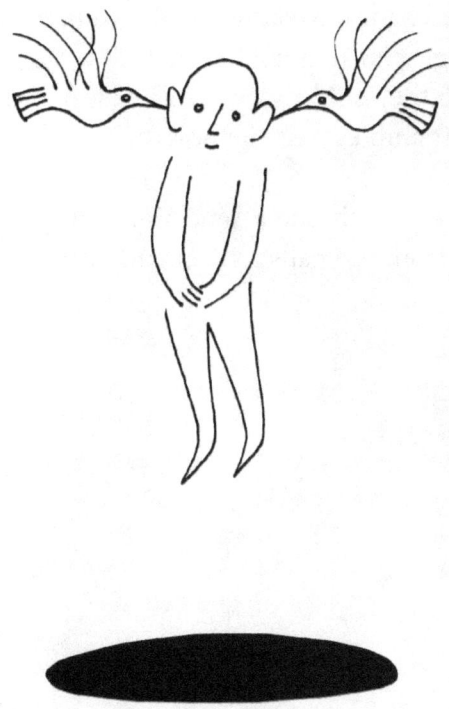

Light Refreshments

The moon has departed and it's nearly breakfast time: gather all the strands of light you can find!

They seize errant sun beams from the low hanging leaves of trees and shake pine tree branches till motes of light drop from each needle point along with sweet warm pollen, which makes them sneeze as they catch both in their cupped hands. Meanwhile, the youngest run out to the clearing, splashing cold clear well-water from silver pails, which they hold above their heads in order to catch the sun as it ambles past the horizon.

Finally, heavy with their reflections, they pluck juicy tangerines from the pails to peel and portion.

Summer

Someone has placed a bowl of oranges in the desert. The bowl is lightest blue and the oranges are a touch of red away from yellow.

The sky holds the dry dunes of the desert under its hands like a prized bug, while the sun shines through a crack in its fingers. The oranges sit in the bowl like little round reminders of rain. No one moves or makes a sound for a long time.

Essence of orange evaporates into fragrant clouds. Someone pitter-patters across the dunes. The rain is coming.

Mirror Day

It is national take your mirror to work day. They giggle as they enter, going round and round in spinning doors. They ride elevators to the top floor and mimic executives.

At lunchtime their fathers and mothers take them to eat reflections and show them off to friends. *My Stevens, the last time I saw your mirror it was only three feet high, this mirror is beginning to look just like you!*

Some envy their vast potential for growth. They learn everything they need to know in an instant. But they have atrocious memory, and they break far too easily.

Sidekicks

The mechanical bull dreams of being a real bull. The real bull is also a freelance detective operating in the rangelands. He has one steadfast partner: the lonesome bartender. For many years, the lonesome bartender and the real bull travel from bar to bar in one-horse towns, winning love and solving local mysteries. Someday soon they will stop needing to close every case and they will head north, to the prairie, side by side.

The maintenance of the mechanical bull is the lonesome bartender's responsibility. He tends to the padded flooring around the mechanical bull so it remains soft and green. He's solved every mystery of the mechanical bull's motor; he makes sure it will run for a long time to come. Someday he will have his own range of soft green grass and a few head of cattle to walk alongside him.

While the bar is closed the mechanical bull awakens as a real bull. He is not the only one. They escape from wood and tarpaper watering holes across the country, trying to find the wide open land. If only they get far enough North: then they will become real bulls forever. At night the lonesome bartenders must round-up their missing mechanical bulls. Every year this seems to happen, a mystery they hope someday to solve.

Glass Boat

for the Peabody Essex Museum in Salem, MA

The artists of the city decided to build a glass boat. It had a glass keel, and a glass mast with glass sails. But what could they do with a glass boat? Out on the ocean it made the sailors nervous. They could see the clouds passing by through the glass sails, but they could not catch the wind. The water waved at their feet, but they could not feel it splashing.

The deck was always smudged with footprints. When the current brought the contraption back to the city's shore it was decided they would hang it in the museum. It looked much better, floating about the ceiling.

But one day the sails caught the current passing through open windows, and the glass boat sailed to the floor. The engineers of the city gathered all the pieces together. They melted the glass and reformed the boat into a giant pyrex measuring cup. The cooks of the city began cracking eggs. One by one they splashed into the glass cup, and tiny bits of shell went up and down on egg white waves.

Hybrid Vigor

Because she was not one for making idle requests it seemed odd for her to say *When the tree springs from your head, I get the apples*; still, he readily agreed to give her whatever fruit might emerge.

Weeks later, when the first roots crowded the follicles of his head, he switched to a clarifying shampoo. The roots thickened, and soon there were nearly as many leaves on his head as hair. She spoke to his hair. She encouraged him to shower more frequently and take long walks in the sun.

When his head blossomed, he sneezed for a week. Bees who approached him became overly enthusiastic. She stroked his head, while jotting down details in her notebook, as the first ponderous fruits formed.

Rolling River

There is always waste in production, but one factory has found a way to dispose of it: each hot, glowing glass bubble shunted to a nearby river, which soon became more marbles than water.

As if bound to their home, the marbles never carried far. They warbled gently as boats passed. Environmentalists and impassioned collectors used their finest mesh nets and buckets to collect specimens for further study. Marbles swirled in circles. Larger marbles pushed the smaller marbles aside, grinding against each other.

The banks of the river became glassy beaches of colorful sand. The marbles rolled up and down the shore, gradually growing smaller, amidst flecks of copper, silver, and bits of brightly dyed feathers.

Our Creations

The science community rejoiced at their newest development: the world's smallest lion; a creature they said would have dominion over a vast menagerie of tiny animals, as soon as they were finished.

The packs of tiny gazelles were already skittish in their pen. The biologists still needed to work on pigmentation kinks with the tiny zebras. Botanists and geologists busied themselves creating a habitat: a savannah as vast as two, or maybe even three, dining room tables, its tall grass reaching almost as high as the rim of a shot glass. They made an underground spring feeding an oasis the size of a teacup. The climatologists perfected three types of arid wind, including one that smelled faintly of acacia.

The world's smallest lion roared. His roar was as loud as a yawn. The conditions made him susceptible to static charge. His mane puffed wildly as he basked beneath a 60-watt light bulb.

Clean Machines

At last, they have built a machine that runs on data. It produces subtle energy; enough to generate a slight shift in an idea, to eliminate forks in a road, to ease a compromise.

In the mountains to the east, they mine continuously for data. The more data they find, the less meaning it has, and thus it generates the least energy. In the mountains to the west, they mine continuously for data. The more data they find, the more meaning it has, and thus it generates unthinkable energy.

Byproducts from the process are saved and further refined for more accurate magic 8 balls. Vast chimneys rise from the factory spewing effluvious and meaningless gases into the atmosphere.

Golem

By the beach of that great lake, we dig barehanded, past forgotten beach toys, past crushed quartz and feldspar, down to the glacial clay deposits, rich with shale which we carefully mound into the stroller. As we've learned, 12 pounds is enough for a modest sized baby, after trimming and firing.

My partner, the potter, suggests that we slip-cast the baby, so if we want to make another baby in the future, we can make one just as good, but I'm old-fashioned: I've always wanted a hand-made baby. I pinch together a tiny nose and ears, then set them aside. She throws a bowl-body on her wheel. I coil build a hollow head, so it won't explode in the kiln.

It's time to stoke the kiln and bisque the baby. We glaze dark, iron-oxide eyes, and grasping fists, but this dry doll doesn't giggle or gurgle. We place it on the mantle with other attempts, and head back to the beach; perhaps this time the unpredictable soda-firing will trigger the crucial reaction.

Wheat Head

In the grain-belt, a company, specializing in genetically modified seeds, grows wheat whose sheaves droop low with pennies. Through careful inter-breeding they have been able to eliminate those with shields or Lincoln monuments. It's unnecessary yet seems like the most natural thing to do.

Breezes go unnoticed, but heavy winds provoke a cheerful, rhythmic clinking. Night after night, the sun presses the pink and orange waves, glints of copper on the die-press of the horizon, leaving behind an oily bronze impression that remains on the grain in the morning.

Sheaves contain up to 50 pennies, hulled by hand and warm to the touch. In some cases, the pennies have not fully formed, instead producing ordinary grain with a thin crust of zinc. Meanwhile, nearby farmers complain of cross-pollination, and the rains smell like metal.

Lightbringers

They kept their angel chained to a post in the subdivision. Its song was so beautiful, all the birds left town in shame. The flowers first flourished, and then wilted in its radiance. Even so, little leaguers rubbed its molting wing tips for good luck. If it really wanted to leave, it would. The others they'd chained had.

Some haunted tourist traps, attuned to the adulation of crowds on pilgrimages. The head of a pin was, in fact, too small a residence, but hundreds set themselves up in disused and rusted locks across the country, or drifted along ley lines during the day, and then dwindled, cocooned between the blossoms of morning glories for the night. Still more found comfort at the bottom of bottles of spirits and then were inadvertently poured as shots.

No one knew if they had plummeted to earth with purpose, to herald an end of times, or some new beginning. They carried no papers, had no citizenship. Sometimes they spoke in whispers, other times great horn blasts. Humanity having found no use for them, they glowed bright and brighter, till all was light.

Stampede at the Premium Outlets

Racks of leather coats collapse, stacks of pre-weathered blue jeans cartwheel like tumbleweeds, turtlenecks are trampled. The foundations tremble before the buildings settle down.

Then the roads leading away from the outlets are packed with buffalo. As they wait for traffic to loosen, they graze on the median strips.

The smells of musk, sweat, and overheated rubber blend as the parking lots fill up with cars, and the cars fill up with leather coats, blue jeans, and turtlenecks.

Expected Delays

The airport food court is a desert, undergoing renovations, and the fast-food burger chain has run out of Happy Meals. Instead, they are selling Tragic Meals. The French fries are soggy, despite their coating of abrasive salt, the kind they use to melt ice on the sidewalk. The sandwich is a bun, inside a bun, inside another bun, slathered in mayonnaise of dubious provenance.

None of the water fountains are working, the planes are grounded, lost in a storm of dust, and the flights have been delayed for months. Women braid each other's hair. Men braid each other's beards.

The smell of the bathrooms is its own forbiddance, nearly a solid wall. The travelers form a circle and begin a rotating dance like the *hora*, circles within circles, tendrils breaking off toward the gates, where they sleep, so they will always be ready to depart. Meanwhile, a child is dowsing for water with a pair of disposable wooden chopsticks.

Autumn

The old clothing decides to throw a party at the back of the wardrobe. Everyone is invited.

Plaid suits tango on wire coat-hangers with sequined black sweaters. Leather boat-shoes snort talcum foot powder, and a pair of khakis staggers about drunk on fermented moth balls. A mob of Hawaiian-print shirts flash everyone and a shock of silver sequins covers the floor.

At last, a fur-liner separates the sleepy, wrinkled revelers. They all agree to meet again next year, same time, same place.

The Deficit

As the sun rises, baristas brew our daily nostrums: espresso mixed with espresso, made near solid with sugar: shot after shot to reduce the size of the dark bags beneath commuters' eyes, and as the sun beats down overhead, petered-out prophets chant bedtime stories in front of mattress discount stores. In the evening, deputized bedtime enforcers gently storm homes, issuing citations for end-table clutter and unmade beds.

The last time we paid down the national sleep debt was during the presidency of Calvin Coolidge, a quieter time, when silver certificates were issued alongside sleep certificates, redeemable through any county treasurer for several hours of pure, unadulterated shut-eye. Of course, this was before the national sleep standard was eliminated to make way for the privatized sleep industry—now we grind woozy lavender powders, mixed with melatonin, and chamomile, and whiskey, as we count sheep, then down from 100, as the deficit steadily increases.

The fed raises rates on pillow-plumping, the House expands tax cuts for nap-rooms, while the Senate debates a sleep-trade agreement with our more well-rested allies. Meanwhile, among financial and dream analysts, rumors spread of children plucked from orphanages and put to work in massive sleep mills, where they must play to the point of exhaustion each day, so they can fulfill their nightly sleep quota.

New Markets

For Michael Martone

It was said that in Indiana, the world's largest repository of hair had been robbed. That thieves had come in the night, and stolen all of the blonde hair, or sometimes it was bleached all the brown hair. Whatever the case, politicians of Indiana began calling in favors.

Within weeks, the Rockettes undertook a cross-country tour calling for all able-haired individuals to buzz, snip, and shave their hair, as a matter of the gravest social security. It became trendy for celebrities to donate their locks in solidarity, or for neighborhoods to hold block-shaving parties. People from other countries began sending in their hair, including over 1000 feet of hair from Canada. The Federal Reserve began issuing 30-year hair-bonds, promising to pay out, in the case of the top tier, close to a hundred feet of thick, wavy hair. There was rampant speculation as to the value of all the donated hair, but it was beyond calculation.

As a result of the demand, the value for hair sky-rocketed. Overnight, economies that foolishly had no skin in the hair game before found their currency devalued. In some neighborhoods it became dangerous for follicly well-endowed individuals to walk alone at night.

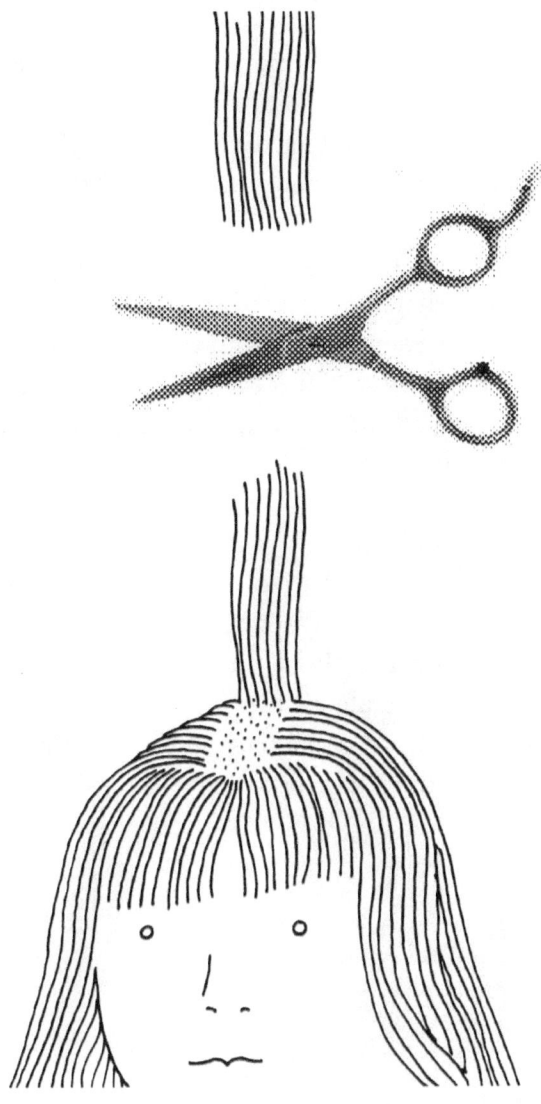

* 75

Where the Bees Are Going II

No place has ever been so emptied. The people left, dust already settled in. For a time the loudest sound was a few porch swings swaying on rusty rings and white paint peeling. There is no one to see what beast will be born of the gradual effects of sunshine and rain, of this pregnant silence.

Then in the heartland, acres of foreclosed homes burst into blossom: stamen stretch between petal-like shutters and a few crumbling chimneys, presenting life to the breeze: beyond broken bricks and windows, a promise of sustenance and shelter.

Later crews rumble down the street, ready to scrape the neighborhood off the horizon. Instead, they find the houses abuzz with activity, not in bedrooms or living rooms, but between walls. Under the sun, homes ooze golden, glowing rivulets. The bulldozers begin, soon becoming mired in sweetness: their metallic yellow glares, futile, in the sticky pools.

To the Heart

There is a faraway island, known for brightly colored and surprisingly textured mosaics, where the people have eyes, not on their heads, but on the bottom of their feet. Naturally, it is important for all business to be conducted reclining.

Lest dust should get in their eyes, they must close them, and so they travel in muffled darkness. Yet these people are known as dedicated explorers. They have mapped miles of the sea floor, and on land they cover as much distance in their minds as underfoot—perhaps more. When at last they reach their destination and raise their feet to the air, it is as if they have just woken from a dream of great industry.

In marriage ceremonies the bride and groom sit, cross-legged, eyes turned inward, closed. As the couple recites the vows their legs unfold: soon soles rest lightly against each other's. Tentatively at first, and then with full confidence, their eyes open.

Minotaur Seeks Real Estate Agent to Find New Maze

He has been in his first maze, a starter maze, a long time, and it has become far too easy for adventurers to find him, unfailingly unearthing him with the fewest possible turns. Not even proper adventurers really: tourists. His fame has outgrown the conundrum of the maze. It's become obvious: now people navigate mazes most of the time.

It must be a better maze, in a quieter neighborhood, though the occasional brave visitor would be welcome. No hardwood floors: they would petrify and then break. Really, most of the masonry options were out. Still worse were the modern institutional options. Who could live cozily in the sterility of a hospital maze, or the flickering lights of an office maze? Now dirt, there's a traditional maze material: limestone, dirt, and roots groping toward other passages.

The real estate agent shows the finest: bright bony catacombs; briny, rust-toned seaport shipping container canyons; or even the forgotten reserves of large state libraries, barely books, a labyrinth of dust wrapped in leather. He'll know it's right when they discover a classic structure within a fully modern, completely renovated entanglement, and are unable to find their way out.

Flotsam

The mattress is going out to sea; it is the last to go. It waited so long on the sand dunes in the wind that the blankets got twisted and itchy and stiff with salt. They headed up the beach to the road, and huddled together, before being saved by a truck heading inland.

The end tables had tumbled, as best two cubes can, crushing sand castles and shells, polishing sea glass, and disrupting the chattered contemplations of sea gulls, before belly-flopping into the water. Their contents: Vaseline, a diaphragm, scrunched clusters of unused Kleenex, a few photos, spare change, dead erasers on pencil stubs, and melted kisses are lost without their home and sink into the shallows.

When the rest have gone, the mattress glides down the beach and into the shallows where it rides indecisively back and forth on the tide. The water laps gently at the floral print and splashes over the top, pooling in twin molds.

Our Hunger

We obsess about making babies. It is all we can think about, this self-propagation. To take the best parts of each other: the proudest, smallest, waving telomeres, and combine them to fulfill our biological imperative. We paint every room in pastel colors, in blushes, and then create new rooms, just so we can paint them too. We are so hungry and so ready, so then we eat our babies.

We can't help it. No one can help it. They are delicious. We make baby stir-fry with baby corn, baby carrots, baby bok choy, baby spinach, baby eggplant. From cocktail swords our teeth envelope tender-sweet baby beets. We puree baby squash for soups and make baby breads from baby zucchini. We feast on lamb and veal. There's enough to share, and so we share every day.

We roast and stuff a suckling pig, and as our drooling friends and family watch we carve off cheery, fatty pieces. Luscious pieces for parents, and daintier, crispier pieces for friends. The meat mugs for the camera: everyone loves it and encourages us to make more babies. We eat and cry and eat some more, because we were so desperate to make a baby, and our baby is delicious.

Our Ineffectual Poetry Lobby

Not for vast farms, big oil, wide trees, or even small bees, but poetry. Not to save the whales, protect prisoners' rights, or so children don't starve, but poetry. For vast anaphora, for big line breaks, reducing regulations on rhymes and fixed form mortgaging. To save the books and preserve personification, for poetry.

Campaign contributions of eraser stubs and replacement typewriter keys, delivered by three blackbirds. Artful packets of thirteen things: how heavy, your coffers now filled with amphibrach. A sheaf of haiku, slipped beneath the door could make a crucial diff'rence.

Brightly colored leaves in bags make up the grassroots effort. Special interests measured out in coffee shops. We do not need to bear this enormous business all alone. Lift up a common meter, for common people, a common refrain to move us. Not unordered, if only for the sake of others, for poetry.

Gravity is No Fan of Growth

The wheel is not an invention to be trifled with. Even walking takes extensive amounts of research.

The distance from a tall parent to the comforting arms of a couch is nearly inconceivable. Avoid excessive jumping and remember as you drive that distance ages faster than anything.

Wave to walkers and children: the future follows alongside them, like a bike just about to lose its training wheels.

ACKNOWLEDGMENTS

Gratefully acknowledged are the following publications, where variations of these poems first appeared:

2RiverView, 580Split, Apocrypha and Abstractions, Artifice Magazine, Beecher's Magazine, Boaat; The Cincinnati Review, Cleaver, Cloaca Magazine, Diagram, DeComp, Ditch, Entropy Magazine, elsewhere, Flyway, Kill Author, The Laurel Review, The Learned Pig, MonkeyBicycle, Mid-American Review, Nashville Review, Opium Online, PANK Online/Print, Paper Darts, Passages North, The Prose Poem Project, Punchnel's, Knock, Santa Clara Review, Subtropics, Yes Poetry, Sweet Wolverine.

Thanks to my family for nurturing a love of stories and poetry, to all my friends, and a wide assortment of colleagues, peers, readers, editors for engaging thoughtfully, providing feedback, coming to readings, inviting me to read, soliciting work, sharing their own work, and offering sustenance and succor, including Lorne, Nona, and Daniel Fienberg; Bill and Ida Fienberg, Norm and Mary Davis, Stephen and Joyce Fienberg, Cynthia and Patrick Maloney, Martin Alex Maloney and Mia Alejandra Gomez Polo, Todd and Monica, and the rest of the Rogers family; Chris

Wong, Sarah Etlinger, Carl Hurvich, Kyle and Dan Brintz, Kieran and Christine Dieter, Kat and Isaac Solomon, Julia Skinner, Christine Alexander, Abigail Cloud, Gabriel Houck, Adam Scheffler, Dan Donoho, Michael Allen Potter, Jay Vithalani, Will Roseliep and Andreea Nicolae, Eric Lenz, J.D. Iripino, Barbara Ohrstrom, Gauge Norris, Rick Dashiell, Seth Stair, Beverly Ballaro, Zach Schomburg, Hadley Griggs, Matthew Schmidt, Dylan Loring, Jon Riccio, Zachary Williams, and Chad Foret, Evan Nichols, Evan Williams, and Ben Niespodziany, Beth Davidson, Alexander Levering Kern, Gina Wironen, Bob Evans, Peggy Silva, Kim Carter, Martha Collins, Lia Purpura, Sylvia Watanabe, David Walker, Robin Hemley, and David Hamilton.

It takes too many people to write a first book to ever acknowledge them all, and over time I know I have forgotten people. To wit, during the poetry unit in my 6th grade English class at Northwestern Elementary School in Leominster, MA, we were discussing sources of inspiration, and one of my classmates said "I'm going to write about Rockwell Pond"—when I said that I wanted to write about it too, they said I could, but only if I thanked them in my first book. I didn't write about Rockwell Pond, and I don't remember your name, but I did write a book, so thank you.

Many institutions, organizations, eateries, and loose affiliations helped make this writing possible including Oberlin College, the University of Iowa, the NWP Bowling Kings, the Lone Tree Mens League, La Muse Inn, Fairgrounds Coffee, elsewhere micro-press, Zero Prestige Pittsburgh, the Lava Step Collective, Sundress Academic for the Arts, the Boston Public Library Map Room, the

Evanston Public Library, Dollop Coffee and the Hoosier Mama Pie Company, Northeastern University's College of Professional Studies, and VCFA's Post Graduate Writing Conference.

For the dogs: there's a bit of Logan, Lilly, Harold, and Millie in "Clockwork Dog." There's also a bit of Pookie, who was a cat-dog.

Special thanks to elsewhere micropress for selecting, editing, and publishing *Old Habits, New Markets* for their chapbook contest, and to Ainsley Romero for agreeing to let a new wave of readers experience her delightful illustrations.

When Amber Sparks reviewed an issue of *Artifice Magazine*, she wrote the kindest things about my work that anyone who didn't know me had ever said. Those words sustained me over years of building worlds. The world is never finished: read *The Unfinished World*.

Brian Evenson is a master of the strange and unsettling, and his work has inspired me to embrace horror in my coziness. We harbor unnatural thoughts in this natural world: read *The Glassy, Burning Floor of Hell*.

In 1983, in Ames, Iowa, when I weighed just about 7 pounds, Michael Martone passed out at my bris; as he read this manuscript, he was preparing to welcome a grandchild. We are all made up of small absurdities: read *Pensees: The Thoughts of Dan Quayle*.

When I heard Jon Riccio poetry at a conference I was blown away. At the airport, we connected over Oberlin tshirts, and he invited me into a poem-a-day group that revitalized my writing practice. Sometimes surrealism is the only way through: read *Agoreagraphy*.

Huge thanks to Ellie Atkinson, Carolyn Czerwinski, Grace Dahl, Dr. Ross Tangedal, and the whole Cornerstone Press team for their appreciation, patience, engagement, and tireless work to put a beautiful book into your hands.

To my readers: this book is called *Where Babies Come From*, but it does not end with a baby. I still don't know where they come from, or how to make one. It's okay if you can't find a baby, make a baby with your body, or bake a baby. It's okay if you can't shape a baby out of sheet metal, clay, or stale gumballs. The baby is not always a baby: you will find and make all the ideas and dreams.

Finally, to Emily, thanks every day for every poem and every pot, for the planned and unplanned adventures, all the birds who've entered and exited our eaves, and all the hope from feathers saved.

ORI FIENBERG is the author of the chapbooks *Old Habits, New Markets* (2020) and *Interim Assistant Dean of Having a Rich Inner Life* (2023). His writing has appeared in *Mid-American Review, Ploughshares, Rattle, Smartish Pace*, and many other journals and anthologies. A graduate of Oberlin College and the University of Iowa's Nonfiction Writing Program, Ori teaches poetry for Northeastern University and lives in Evanston, Illinois.

www.ingramcontent.com/pod-product-compliance
Lightning Source LLC
Chambersburg PA
CBHW031441120626
46545CB00006B/2512